A DEADLY COBRA

TOM JACKSON

ANIMAL INSTINCTS

WAYLAND

First published in 2011 by Wayland
Copyright © 2011 Wayland

Wayland
338 Euston Road
London NW1 3BH

Wayland Australia
Level 17/207 Kent Street
Sydney NSW 2000

Editor: Julia Adams
Designer: Paul Cherrill
Picture researcher: Tom Jackson

Jackson, Tom.
  A deadly cobra. -- (Animal instincts)
  1. Cobras--Behavior--Juvenile literature
  2. Cobras--Life cycles--Juvenile literature.
  I. Title II. Series
  597.9'642-dc22

ISBN 978 0 7502 6589 8

The author and publisher would like to thank
the following agencies for allowing these pictures
to be reproduced:
All images and graphic elements: Shutterstock, apart
from: p. 1: Dreamstime; p. 2 (bottom): iStock; p. 4 (cobra
and rattlesnake outlines): iStock; pp. 6–7: NHPA/Daniel
Heuchlin; p. 9 (top): Dreamstime; p. 9 (bottom): Dorling
Kindersley; pp. 10–11,main image: Simon Hosking/
FLPA; p. 11 (top): Aqua Image/Alamy; pp. 12–13: Imag-
esBroker/Imagebroker/FLPA; p. 13 (In the know inset):
Juniors Bildarchiv/Alamy; pp. 14–15: George Logan/
Corbis; p. 15 (inset): Claus Meyer; p. 16: naturepl.com/
Mary McDonald; p. 17: naturepl.com/Mary McDonald;
p. 18 (inset): Mattias Klum/Getty; p. 19: NHPA/Daniel
Heuchlin; p. 20 (top): Photoshot Holdings Ltd/Alamy;
p. 20 (bottom): Jeffrey L. Rotman/Corbis; p. 22: Justin
Locke/National Geographic Society/Corbis; pp. 24–25:
Tara Todras-Whitehill/Reuters/Corbis; p. 24 (inset):
Tara Todras-Whitehill/Reuters/Corbis; p. 25 (inset):
Stuart Corlett/Alamy; pp. 26–27: NHPA/Photoshot; p.
27 (inset): Joel Satore/Getty; pp. 28–29: Jeffrey L. Rot-
man/Corbis; p. 29 (top): iStock; p. 29 (bottom): Jeffrey L.
Rotman/Corbis;

Should there be any inadvertent omission, please apply
to the publisher for rectification.

Printed in China

Wayland is a division of Hachette Children's Books,
an Hachette UK company.
www.hachette.co.uk

CONTENTS

scary snakes

Are you afraid of snakes? Many people fear these animals, even though some are harmless. But be warned: cobras are very dangerous. With little more than a hiss of warning, these snakes give poisonous bites that can kill a person.

There are 25 types of cobra. They live in **Africa** and **Asia**. Like all reptiles, cobras are **cold-blooded**. They do not make their own body heat. Instead, they rely on the sun to keep them warm.

Strong, twisty body.

SIZING UP SNAKES

Indian cobra

Rattlesnake

Reticulated python

Reticulated python:
Length: 10 m; weight: up to 200 kg

Rattlesnake:
Length: 1.5 m weight: 4 kg

Indian cobra:
Length: 2 m; weight: 9 kg

Average human:
Height: 1.7 m; weight: 70 kg

Narrow tail.

Hood

Cobras have wide 'hoods', which are used as a warning sign to stay away. Indian cobras have a marking on their hoods that look like a pair of glasses. That is why these snakes are also known as spectacled cobras.

'Spectacles' on hood.

Hatching out

Cobras hatch from eggs. The baby snakes use a spike on their snouts to crack through the shell. This 'egg tooth' falls off just after they slither out of the egg.

My mum and dad left before I hatched. But I did not need their help, because I could catch enough insects to eat by myself.

A baby cobra is about 30 cm long when it hatches.

Eggs

Many different animals lay eggs. An egg protects an animal while it develops.

Reptile eggs have shells that are leathery and waterproof.

Birds lay eggs with hard shells. Their shape means they always roll in circles, so they never roll away from the nest.

Amphibian eggs, such as frog spawn, don't have shells. They are laid in wet places, so they don't dry out.

Egg

WoW!

Baby cobras already have enough **venom** to kill **prey** when they hatch.

Silent hunter

As cobras grow, they become more venomous. They move so silently that their prey cannot hear them.

Now that I have grown to my full length, my body is very powerful. I am 2 metres long and I can move at 16 kilometres per hour without making a noise. That's the speed of an average person's sprint.

The **scales** on the belly of cobras are hooked. They grip the ground as the snake pushes itself along.

I look everywhere for food. I even climb up trees and swim in swamps. I don't find much food in deep water like this river, but I can swim across it easily enough to find food on the other side.

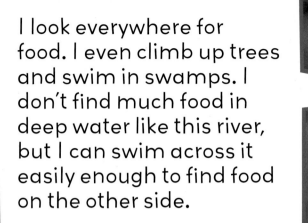

Cobras swim at the surface. They do not dive under the water to look for food.

On the move

Cobras move in different ways, depending on the ground they are on.

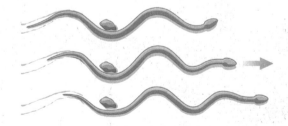

In trees: The snake bends its body into large curves. Then it pushes its head forwards and pulls its body close by bending it into curves again.

Rough ground and water: The cobra's body waves from side to side. It pushes its curved body against the rough ground or water to move itself forward.

My patch

Cobras eat a lot of mice. Many mice live close to humans, because it is easy for them to find food in houses. They also eat seeds and crops they find in farmers' fields.

I don't really have a home. I rest wherever there is a good place to hide. I travel through forests and fields. Sometimes I go into houses by mistake when I am hunting mice.

Cobras are often seen on the edge of fields.

This swamp of mud and grass looks like a good place to hunt. I might find a frog or a rat. Sometimes people come here and **harvest** the plants. I always hide from them.

Cobras often hunt in rice fields or paddies. There are a lot of rats there nibbling on the rice plants in the shallow water.

IN THE KNOW

Cobras often live where one **habitat** changes into another, such at the edge of a forest. This means that they can catch prey from two habitats.

Getting a taste

When cobras get on the trail of a meal, they use their sense of smell. But snakes do not sniff the air. They taste it instead.

When I hunt for food, I flick my tongue in and out to catch the smell of prey. I can even tell where smells are coming from. This means I can hunt in the dark, too.

Large, round eyes see well in the dark.

Forked tongue

Smells are made up of chemicals in the air. The chemicals stick to the tips of the snake's forked tongue. The snake slots the forks into a smelling organ on the roof of its mouth. The tip with the most chemicals is the one that is nearer to where the smell is coming from. So the snake heads in that direction.

Smelling organ

Animals with amazing tongues

Many animals use their tongues in ways that humans can't.

Blue-tongue skink: Its bright blue tongue scares off attackers.

Hummingird: This bird's long, brushy tongue licks up flower pollen.

Dolphins: As they have no nose, dolphins smell with their tongues!

Death bite

When the cobra spots its prey, it silently creeps as close as it can. It uses its sharp eyes to get into the best position to attack.

WOW!

A cobra's venom is so strong, it can kill an elephant with one bite.

Venom

Cobra venom is made from _saliva_, the same liquid that wets your mouth. The difference is that there are chemicals in the venom that stop the heart and other parts of the body from working. When a cobra bites, the venom enters the victim's body through the hollow fangs.

The fangs are long teeth. They are folded flat when the snake's mouth is closed.

My attacks are quick and fierce! A single bite is all it takes for me to kill a mouse. Then I hold it in my mouth so it does not run away before the venom has had a chance to work. The mouse dies within seconds.

A long, slow lunch

Snakes cannot chew their food. They also can't rip off chunks, because they would need to use legs or arms to tug at the flesh. So snakes have to swallow every meal whole.

I always swallow prey headfirst, otherwise the legs would get in the way. My mouth can stretch very wide. This mouse is bigger than my own head, but I am able to swallow it anyway.

Cobra venom softens mice and makes them easier to swallow.

A snake's lower jaw bone can move down and sideways to fit around prey. Then the snake can pull in and gulp down food with the help of its strong throat muscles. Cobras do not eat very often — once every few weeks is enough.

WOW!

A cobra eating a mouse is like a person eating a watermelon in one gulp.

I can feel the mouse in my throat. It looks like a large bulge. It will slowly move down my body, getting smaller as I **digest** it.

Danger approaches

Snakes can't hear. But they can feel even tiny **vibrations** in the ground. This is how they sense when enemies are close.

Silent enemies

*One of the few things cobras cannot hear is other cobras approaching – they are just too **stealthy**. That is a problem because Indian cobras are **cannibals**. They prey on each other.*

Indian cobra eating another Indian cobra.

Cobras can feel the vibrations that footsteps make.

19

Facing the enemy

The cobra's smallest and deadliest enemy is the mongoose. These animals can kill cobras within minutes. A cobra will die if it doesn't escape the attack of a mongoose.

This mongoose is so quick. I try to bite, but I keep missing. It's biting me, though. I need to get away if I can.

Sometimes the only reason why a cobra survives a mongoose attac is the arrival of a mongoose **predator**, such as a leopard.

Snake protection

Mongooses live all over Asia and Africa. Some people keep these tough little hunters as pets to protect them from snakes in their home.

A pet mongoose eating a cobra.

The mongoose is not affected by cobra venom. It attacks a cobra by biting it with its sharp teeth.

meeting humans

Cobras see humans as their enemies and normally try to hide from them. But when cobras and humans meet, a cobra might attack if it feels threatened.

The cobra's hood forms when the snake stretches its ribcatch outwards.

IN THE KNOW

If cobras feel trapped, they can attack very quickly. Many thousands of people get bitten every year.

Sometimes when I chase a mouse, I get trapped in a house. If a human finds me, I make myself look as big as possible, so I look scary and don't get attacked.

Charming trick

Cobras are too dangerous to be kept as pets, but in parts of India, people called snake charmers perform with cobras. They keep the cobras in dark baskets. When the charmer takes off the lid, the cobra is disturbed by the light and rises up. The snake sees the charmer's swaying pipe and follows its movements, ready to strike at it. It looks like the snake is dancing, but it cannot hear the music.

captured and milked

When cobras become a threat to humans, the snake catcher is called. It is very dangerous to catch a cobra. Most people leave it to the experts.

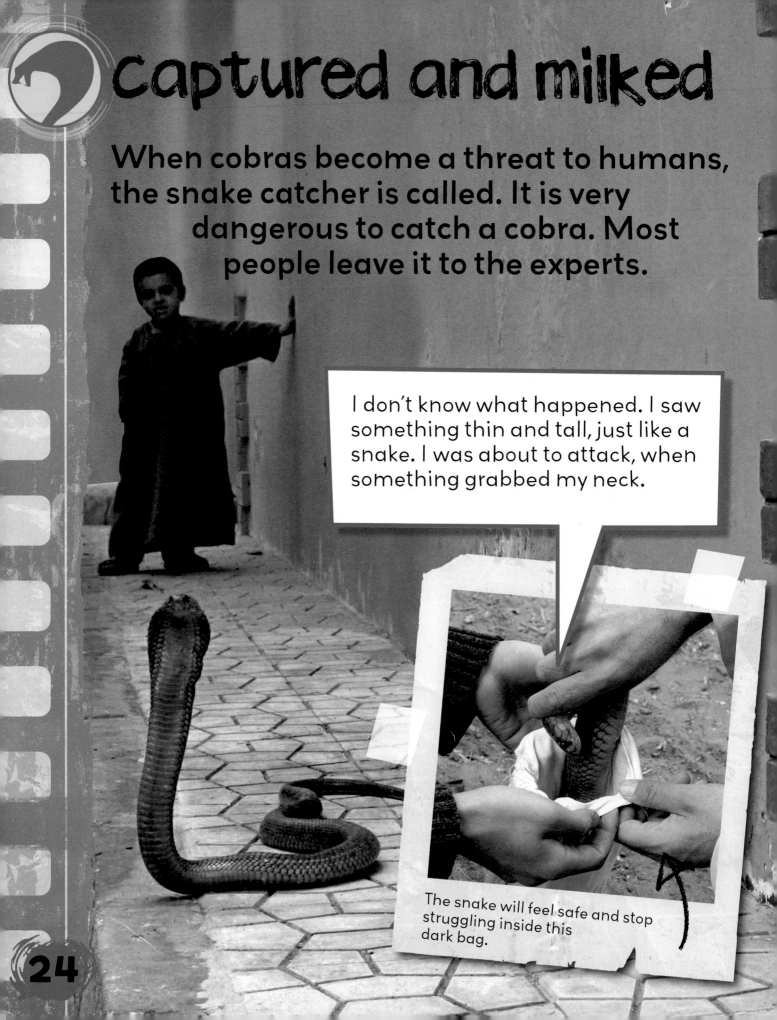

I don't know what happened. I saw something thin and tall, just like a snake. I was about to attack, when something grabbed my neck.

The snake will feel safe and stop struggling inside this dark bag.

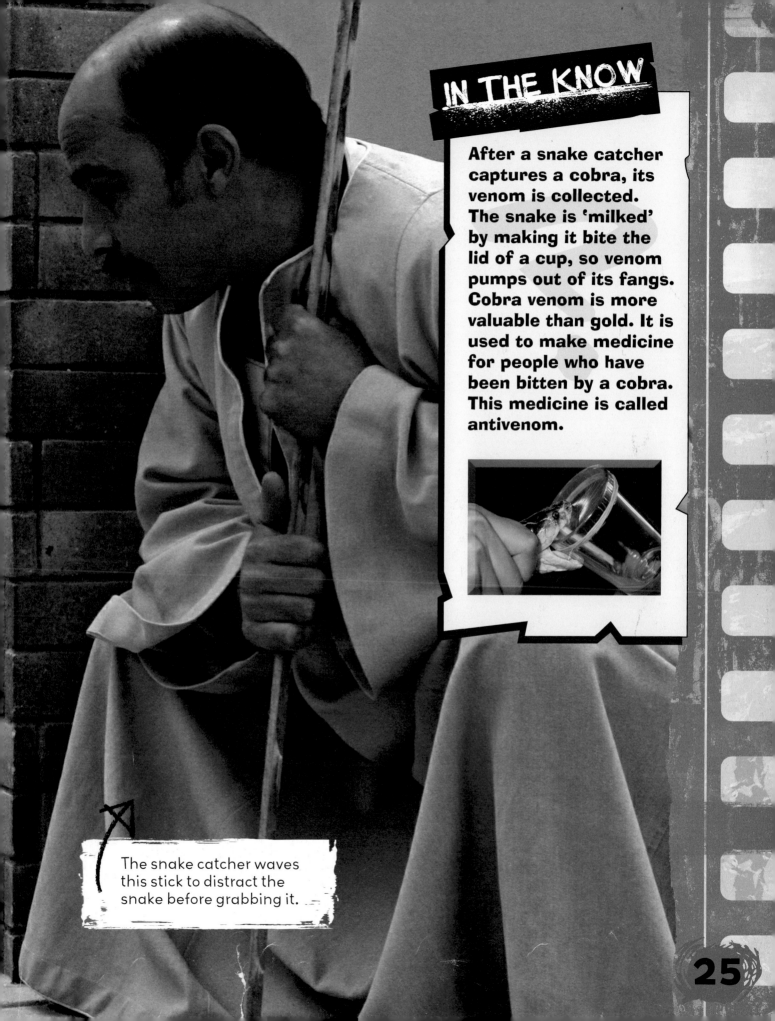

After a snake catcher captures a cobra, its venom is collected. The snake is 'milked' by making it bite the lid of a cup, so venom pumps out of its fangs. Cobra venom is more valuable than gold. It is used to make medicine for people who have been bitten by a cobra. This medicine is called antivenom.

The snake catcher waves this stick to distract the snake before grabbing it.

25

Cobra scales don't stretch. This is why they shed their skin as they grow. **Female** cobras also shed their skin before they lay their eggs.

I'm very clean now I've shed my skin. It is time to lay my eggs. I've chosen a quiet place for them. They will take some time to hatch, and I will stay here to keep them safe.

Giving birth

Some snakes are born. This rattlesnake carried her eggs inside her body. The baby hatched inside her before she gave birth to it.

Mother rattlesnake

Baby rattlesnake

Cobra eggs take 50 days to hatch. The mother leaves before the eggs hatch. She is so hungry by then that she might eat her babies.

Saving snakes

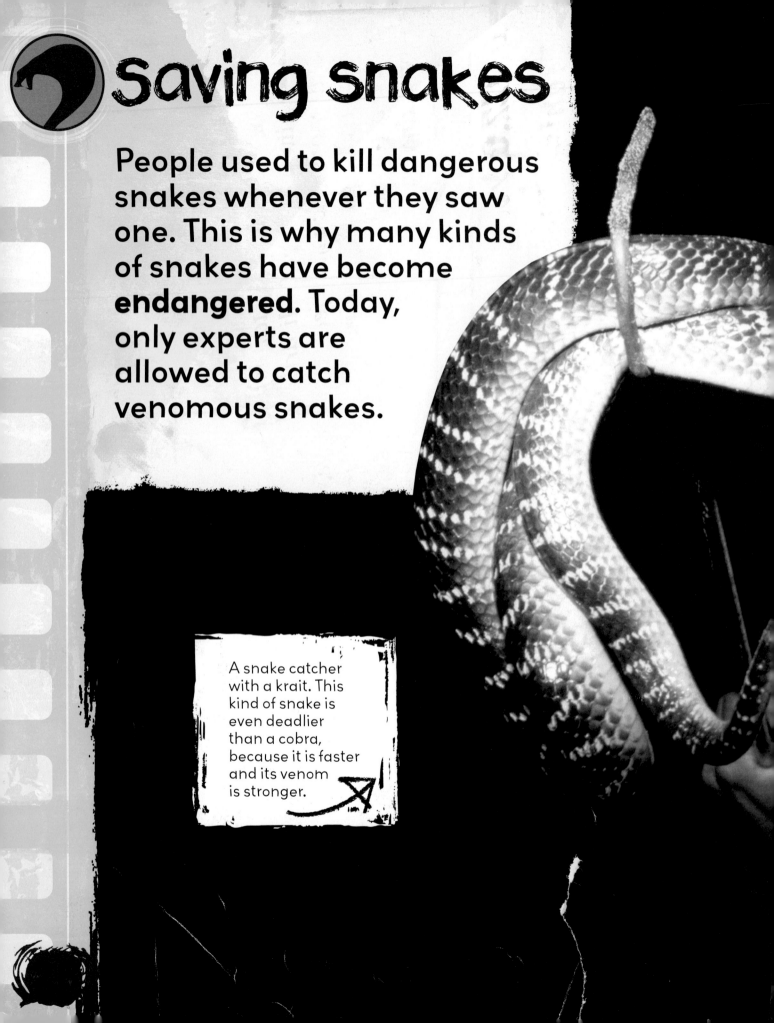

People used to kill dangerous snakes whenever they saw one. This is why many kinds of snakes have become **endangered**. Today, only experts are allowed to catch venomous snakes.

A snake catcher with a krait. This kind of snake is even deadlier than a cobra, because it is faster and its venom is stronger.

Snake skin is often made into leather. People used to kill wild snakes for their skin. Today, the leather is made from snakes grown on snake farms.

The Irulas, a tribe from southern India, are paid to catch cobras. They learn from an early age how to handle venomous snakes.

QUIZ

1) Indian cobras are the longest snakes in the world. True or false?

2) Snakes use the tongue to a) signal to each other b) 'taste' the air c) clean their eyes?

3) Why is the mongoose one of the cobra's deadliest enemies?

4) Cobras are blind. True or flase?

5) Can snakes swim?

6) Snakes always chew their food before swallowing. True or false?

7) Why are cobras 'milked'?

Answers:
1) False, reticulated pythons are five times as long as cobras.
2) b – cobras use their tongue to 'taste' the air
3) Mongooses are not affected by cobra venom.
4) False.
5) Yes, snakes can swim.
6) False.
7) Cobras are 'milked' to collect their venom. The venom is used to make a medicine called antivenom.

GLOSSARY

Africa A large continent, or area of land, that is in a warm part of the world. Africa includes countries like Egypt, Kenya and Nigeria.

Asia The biggest continent on Earth which stretches half way around the world. Asia includes countries like India, China and Japan.

average Halfway between the maximum (very large) and minimum (very small) sizes.

cannibal An animal that eats other members of its own species or group – even eating its own children or parents.

cold-blooded When an animal cannot heat itself up but has to lie in the sun to get warm.

digest To break up food into its simple ingredients that can be taken in by an animal and used to power the body.

endangered When a type of animal is in danger of dying out.

habitat The place where animals live and find food. Most animals live in one type of habitat.

harvest The time when farmers gather in the corn, fruit or vegetables they have grown.

predator An animal that hunts for other animals and then kills them for food; all snakes are predators.

prey An animal that is hunted or killed by another for food.

saliva The slimy water that keeps the mouth wet; snakes and some other animals have poisonous saliva.

scales Hard, waterproof plates that cover a snake's body and the skin of other reptiles.

stealthy Quiet and secret, so as not to be noticed.

venom A poison produced by snakes and other animals that is pumped into the body to kill prey and attackers.

vibrations Shakes and wobbles that travel through the ground, water or air.

Index

Animal Instincts

Contents of titles in the series